"A spiritual landscape done in silverpoint. It is a delicate portrayal of that winter of the soul which suddenly gives promise of spring."

The Listener

WINTER SOLSTICE

WALMER POETRY

The Pelican Island by James Montgomery

Poems by Katherine Mansfield

Victory for the Slain by Hugh Lofting

Nakiketas and other poems by May Sinclair

Winter Solstice by Gerald Bullett

WINTER SOLSTICE

by

Gerald Bullett

SANDNESS
MICHAEL WALMER
2024

Winter Solstice first published 1943

© Gerald Bullett 1943

This edition published 2024

by

Michael Walmer
Little Pradies
13a Melby
Sandness
Shetland ZE2 9PL.

ISBN 978-1-7635656-0-9 hardcover

Be wary that thou conceive not bodily that which is meant ghostly, although it be spoken in bodily words, as be these.

THE CLOUD OF UNKNOWING

I

In secret, in the all-creative silence,

Behind the mask, under the crust of winter,

Love lives unmanifest, pain stirs,

Desire cries in the night unappeasable.

Unappeasable the isolated spirit

Waking alone, the self in the seed,

The minute particle, the bubble ego,

Waking alone to its own aloneness:

Till, in the appointed season,

As it were sunseeds sepulchred in earth

And from that tomb

Leaping to communion with their parent light,

Love, longing beyond mortal measure,

Breaks into flower and leaf.

                                Spirit knows

Its own: in the multitudinous illusion

Of time, in its own myriad imaginings

Incarnate, the eternal seeks and finds itself:

In earth air fire water, beast and bird,

Beetle and bug and mayfly, all that inhabits

Day's wide welkin, bowl of abundancy,

Or sky of sable bursting into coruscation

Of moon and stars.

                             In the lithe tracery

Of bare trees on winter's callow sky,

In bird flying, frog spawning, gelid fish

Cosily pillowed in cold shadow under

The thin pane of the pond my window looks on,

In the hieroglyph of heaven, the vein'd leaf,

The cosmic phantasy and the microcosmic

Spirit of man, moved to infinite desire and

Dark with the shadow of doom long foreknown,

There runs the signature of a nameless mystery

Too near for knowledge and too far for finding,

Save in the wordless motions of the heart.

Curt ecstasy, bitter fulfilment

Wounding wonder of dissevered union,

When every moment's marriage of true hearts

Involves its own divorce, which hands and lips,

Fondly consenting, strive against in vain:

Such are our loves.

Brief love, because brief life. The candle's out

Ere yet the match that kindled it is cold,

And they are left to mourn whom in their turn,

And in no distant day, others must mourn for,

Shadows lamenting shadows. We emerge

As moments in a dream, for whom, momently,

The bell tolls: for whom the bell tolls.

II

Even we, the middling sedentary men,

Middling in worldly status and dignity,

Whose condition would be accounted comfort by
some

And by others regarded as a hairshirt

Intolerably irksome, we whom Success,

Pre-eminent explorer of suburban avenues

And tireless turner of imperial stones,

Has never much regarded, nor we her,

Though had she more inclined herself towards us

We should not I doubt have been deterred

By her unimpeachable vulgarity

From the bosom where our betters lie buried
before us:

Even we, even I, I in my middle years

Who have so far survived, with others of my age,

The two wars of our incomparable time,

Even we have known pain and fear

(Small pain, much fear, since the heart is a child)

And we understand something, though little
enough,

Of the long night and the breaking heart.

I have lain a long time in the darkness of the
spirit,

Hearing my own heart, and yours who suffer.

And to you, wherever you are, who sit fingering

The unanswerable letter, you who listen

For the stilled laughter, the uncoming footstep,

You patterning in time, as God knows all must,

The eternal crucifixion that is love,

To you I bring my pennyworth of pain

In brotherly token. It is all I have.

The agony of the flesh let no man belittle,

But the agony of the flesh must have an end.

The agony of the spirit is the agony or terror

Of the going out of lights, one after one.

But if you untie the hard knot of the will,

Something happens that is like a miracle.

The last star quenched, the last light gone,

The last and longest and cruellest, which is hope,

Darkness like a rose dawns at the still centre,

And the spirit is home.

It is possible that death is something like this.

I am not of those who know about these things,

But I have lain a long time in the darkness

And here I make report.

III

In the heart of the lotus, at the still centre,

There is peace.

Not poppied oblivion, not the dim dream,

Not the spent swimmer on the salt shore

Lying prone, not the deep repose

After perfected passion, not the luxury

Of arriving from the cold climb

At the inn and the inglenook and the spread table,

Not the drowsy pleasure

Of tiredness aching out of warm limbs,

Not folding of the hands for sleep,

Not dream, not trance,

Not slumber nor the visitations of slumber:

Not these, but a quietness,

Wherein the senses five

In the lens of the spirit are made one,

And made alive.

IV

Now from this inwardness walled in with books

I carry my thoughts into the luminous

Wide room under the sky. On field and road,

On farm and folding downs, the sky has cast

His fleece, and mirth lies fallow with the land.

The bells of Christ are silent. Winter and war

Bring havoc to the heart: which yet believes,

So still the day with blithe expectancy,

That of the wintered earth's long chastisement

New strength and beauty may be brought to birth

And ancient joy return,

So still the world this winter noon.

V

So still the world this winter noon,

So sparkling-cold and still,

Of quietness the heart

Could take her fill.

Upon the shallow snow

Clear rang my careful tread.

Summer had died, long ago,

But was not dead

While from the lattice thorn,

To chide my lingering doubt,

Lively with faith and fear

A feathered eye looked out,

And on the powdered verge,

Where road gives way to grass

For others' coming and going,

Many a printing was

Of blackbird, of wren:

Who burn away their blood,

Even as we,

To ends not understood.

So rare the fallen fleece of the sky,

So far the noise of men,

Myself for a musing moment

Was blackbird, was wren.

VI

In a season of rejoicing there is much to
remember

Of sadness. At the feast of friends

There are always — whether of living or dead —

Ghosts in attendance, and as time goes on,

With this or that one away, who came often, or
who

Sat for many a year in the window-seat

Knitting the past into remembered patterns,

With guests gone and children no longer children,

The ghosts come to outnumber the rest of us.

You could almost tell the years of a man's age,

The quality and measure of his heart's maturity,

By the ghosts that gather, year by year, at his
table,

In the season of the celebration of the myth.

For unto us a child is born, unto is a son is given,

Venite adoremus dominum.

A lovely legend carries its own warrant:

But myth in the soil of a literal mind

Grows rank, taking to itself

All that else would nourish the spirit of man

Hungry for the silence of its native mystery.

Omnia exeunt in mysterium

And that alone is real which is alone

From everlasting to everlasting.

That alone is real which cannot be known,

For it is the knowing.

That alone is real which cannot be thought,

For it is the thinking.

When you came to your cradle, that was there

Which is nothing, nameless, nowhere, everywhere.

VII

Cast words away. In secret, in silence,

That which no thought can compass nor tongue
tell,

The heart knows.

Too far to be found, too near to be known,

Meaning eludes our nets, the mystery

Cannot be stated. Not that words falter:

Falter they may but do not falter enough.

Even the shyest among them, the half-heard

Disavowal, hint of qualification,

Is overbold: all words are overbold:

With saying and gainsaying, myth and
metaphysic

They crowd the temple. If my words were clear

They were too clear: if cloudy, still too clear:

And, having said, I cast my words away.

Time gathers in day's eye, the things we speak

Go and are gone, fall as petals fall

Summer by summer till the doom of time

To dream desireless in the long grass,

Fade as the circling voices of the sea

Fade in the mind when the dark angel comes

With all-consuming quiet, warm and good

As honeyed hawthorn loading April air

Wave upon wave, to give our senses sleep.

From world withdrawn the inner mind awakes:

Darkness without, the lamp is lit within.

Words vanish, thought dissolves,

And from the shadowy dissolving husk

Meaning emerges, and the host is here.

VIII

Nothing, nameless, nowhere, everywhere:

When you came to your cradle I was there.

Creaturely kind in lion and lamb,

In star shining, in bud breaking, I am.

I am fear and faith, the fall and the contrition,

The aching hope and the wry fruition,

The bread of communion, the wine of bliss,

The living water of quietness,

The corn ripening, the linnet calling,

The first feathers of dusk falling,

The comrade, the lover, the casual friend.

I am that you shall find at the day's end.

www.ingramcontent.com/pod-product-compliance
Ingram Content Group UK Ltd.
Pitfield, Milton Keynes, MK11 3LW, UK
UKHW020235040125
452912UK00002B/5